NATIONAL GEOGRAPHIC

School Publishing

Geography

Ari Brennan

PICTURE CREDITS
Cover, 1, 2, 4, 5, 8 (below and right above), 9 (left below and right above), 10, 11, (right), 12, 13, 14 (left), 17, 18, 19, 20 (left and right above), 21, 22, 23, Photolibrary.com; 15, 16, 20 (right below) APL/Corbis; 9 (right below), 11 (left below), Alamy; 6, 22, Map created by Equator Graphics for National Geographic's *Map Essentials* program

Produced through the worldwide resources of the National Geographic Society, John M. Fahey, Jr., President and Chief Executive Officer; Gilbert M. Grosvenor, Chairman of the Board; Nina D. Hoffman, Executive Vice President and President, Books and Education Publishing Group.

PREPARED BY NATIONAL GEOGRAPHIC SCHOOL PUBLISHING
Steve Mico, Executive Vice President and Publisher, Children's Books and Education Publishing Group; Marianne Hiland, Editor in Chief; Lynnette Brent, Executive Editor; Michael Murphy and Barbara Wood, Senior Editors; Nicole Rouse, Editor; Bea Jackson, Design Director; David Dumo, Art Director; Shanin Glenn, Designer; Margaret Sidlosky, Illustrations Director; Matt Wascavage, Manager of Publishing Services; Sean Philpotts, Production Manager.

MANUFACTURING AND QUALITY MANAGEMENT
Christopher A. Liedel, Chief Financial Officer; Phillip L. Schlosser, Vice President; Clifton M. Brown III, Director.

BOOK DEVELOPMENT
Ibis for Kids Australia Pty Limited.

Published by the National Geographic Society
1145 17th Street, N.W.
Washington, D.C. 20036-4688

Product No. 4W1005070
ISBN-13: 978-1-4263-5066-5
ISBN-10: 1-4263-5066-X

2010 2009 2008 2007 2006
1 2 3 4 5 6 7 8 9 10 11 12 13 14 15

Printed in China

Contents

Think and Discuss

a park in a city

a desert

4

Earth has many different places. Describe the places in these pictures.

a valley

mountains and a lake

a beach

5

What Is Geography?

Geography is the study of places on Earth. It includes the study of Earth's land, water, and people.

Maps are important in geography. They help to show what Earth is like.

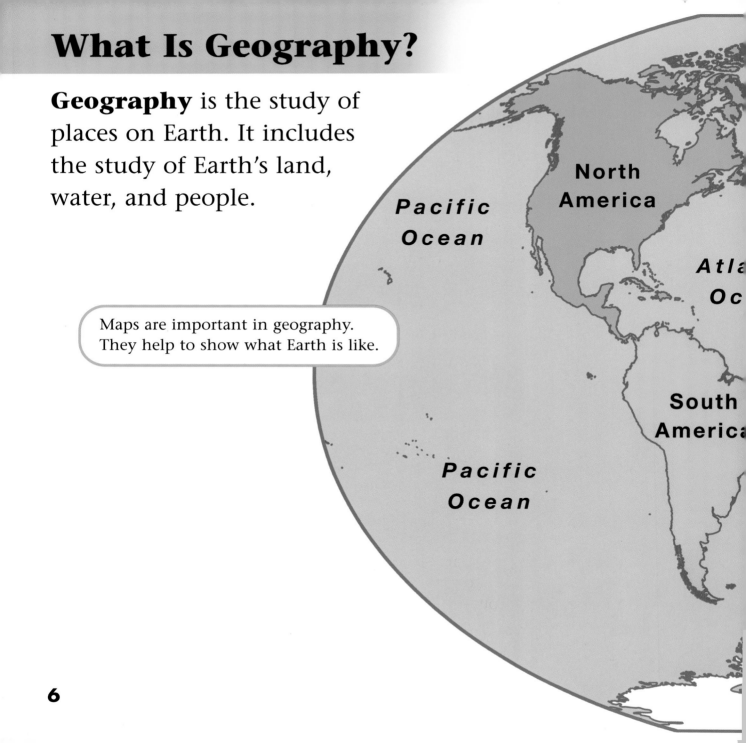

Pacific
Ocean

North
America

Atla
Oc

Pacific
Ocean

South
America

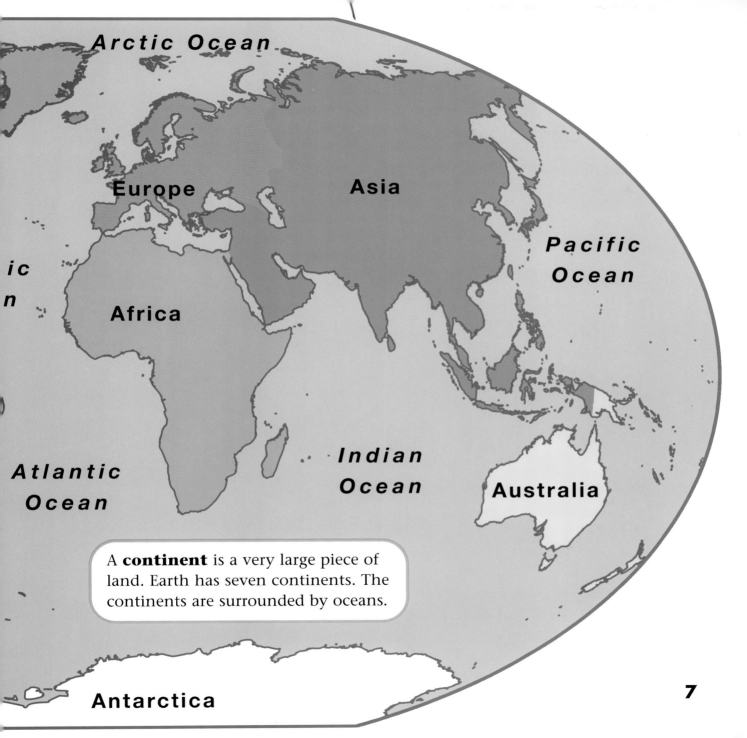

Arctic Ocean

Europe

Asia

Pacific
Ocean

ic
n

Africa

Atlantic
Ocean

Indian
Ocean

Australia

A **continent** is a very large piece of
land. Earth has seven continents. The
continents are surrounded by oceans.

Antarctica

Landforms

A **landform** is the shape of the land. Mountains, hills, and valleys are landforms. Plains and cliffs are landforms, too.

A plain is a large area of flat country, with few or no trees. Some plains make good farmland.

A cliff is a high, steep area of rock. Many cliffs are along water or in the mountains.

A mountain is a very tall area of land. A valley is a low place between mountains or hills.

Landform Extremes

Mount Everest, in Nepal, is the highest mountain on Earth. It is 29,017 feet tall.

The Dead Sea is a lake between Israel and Jordan. The shore, or edge, of the Dead Sea is the lowest place on Earth.

9

Bodies of Water

Earth has many **bodies of water**. Oceans are the largest. Rivers, lakes, and marshes are bodies of water, too.

Rivers flow into other bodies of water. This river flows into the ocean.

The largest ocean on Earth is the Pacific Ocean.

Lakes are bodies of water surrounded by land. There is an island in this lake.

A marsh is a low area of very wet ground.

Climate

Climate is what the weather is like over a long period of time. Climate includes how much rain falls, and how hot or cold a place is. Different places have different climates.

Some mountains are covered in snow all year.

Tropical places are usually warm all year long. Some tropical places have rainy seasons and dry seasons.

Deserts are dry places. They are often hot during the day and cold at night.

Climate Extremes

Death Valley, California, is one of the hottest places on Earth. The hottest temperature ever recorded there was 134 degrees Fahrenheit.

Antarctica is the coldest place on Earth. The temperature is about −125 degrees Fahrenheit in the winter.

People Depend on the Earth

Earth's geography affects people. Rivers, oceans, and lakes provide water and transportation. Land provides places to live and grow food. Climate can determine how people live.

These people grow food on the sides of mountains. They gather wood for fires.

Some people who live in wet places build houses on stilts.

This river is used to move goods and people to different places.

People Use the Earth

Natural resources are important to people. A natural resource is something from the Earth that people use. Water is a natural resource. Trees and soil are natural resources, too.

Wood from trees is used to build houses and furniture. Wood is also made into paper and cardboard.

Many natural resources come from under the ground. This is a coal mine. Coal is used to make electricity.

People get food from the water. This net is full of fish from the ocean.

People Change the Earth

Sometimes people change the Earth.
They dig and move land. They cut down trees.
They also change bodies of water.
People change the Earth for many reasons.

People dug through land to make the Panama Canal. The **canal** connects the Atlantic and Pacific Oceans.

When forests disappear, the land and climate can change. People can plant new trees to replace the ones that were cut down.

Special Places on Earth

People protect some special places on Earth. In the United States, national parks are areas that are protected by the government. Some national parks have amazing landforms and many wild animals. This picture shows Yosemite National Park, in California.

Talk about landforms, bodies of water, and climate. How do these things affect people?

body of water

climate

continent

geography

landform

natural resource

Glossary

body of water (page 10)
A large area of water such as an ocean, lake, or river
A river is a body of water.

canal (page 18)
A long, narrow body of water that is made by people
The Panama Canal connects the Atlantic and the Pacific Oceans.

climate (page 12)
What the weather is like over a long period of time
A desert has a dry climate.

continent (page 7)
A very large piece of land
Earth has seven continents.

geography (page 6)
The study of places on Earth
When people learn about places on Earth, they are studying geography.

landform (page 8)
The shape of the land
A mountain is a landform.

natural resource (page 16)
Something from the Earth that people use
Trees are a natural resource.

Index